how to help a
child cope with
grief

D1368420

Dedication
This book is dedicated to my husband Guy, and my three children
Clare, Jane and Peter and my two step-children Charmian and Dan,
all of whom have experienced the death of a parent.

About the author
Janice Perkins is an education consultant who has worked with
children as a teacher and youth worker. She now advises teachers
and adults who work with children in the area of personal, social
and health education. She is married with five children and is
surviving breast cancer.

Acknowledgements
Ian Hanks, manager of A E Smith and Son, funeral directors in
Swindon, Wiltshire

With grateful thanks to all those who shared their experiences of
grief and bereavement with me, and contributed to the quotes
throughout the book.

how to help a
child
cope with
grief

a book for adults
who live and
work with
bereaved children

janice perkins

foulsham
LONDON • NEW YORK • TORONTO • SYDNEY

foulsham

The Publishing House, Bennetts Close, Cippenham, Slough,
Berkshire, SL1 5AP, England

Foulsham books can be found in all good bookshops and direct from
www.foulsham.com

ISBN: 978-0-572-03309-5

Copyright © 2007 Janice Perkins

Cover photograph © Superstock

Illustrations by Ruth Murray

A CIP record for this book is available from the British Library

The moral right of the author has been asserted

Printed by Creative Print and Design, Wales

Contents

Introduction

We can't prevent the birds of sorrow from landing on our shoulder. We can prevent them nesting in our hair.

Old Chinese proverb

This book was written to help adults who care for or work with children who have been bereaved or who are facing the death of someone close to them.

I acknowledge that some of the adults may also be bereaved and are having to cope with their own grief as well as supporting their children. Other adults, maybe professionals working with children, may find that the child's grief awakens unresolved grief within themselves. Others' response may be that they don't know what to say and therefore say nothing, leaving both themselves and the bereaved child feeling isolated.

Fear and feelings of inadequacy can stop adults from helping their children come to terms with the fact that loss and bereavement are an inevitable part of our lives. Death is still a taboo subject in our society and, while not wanting to go back to Victorian times when death and mourning was very public, I feel it is so important that we help our children both face and cope with such a powerful event in their lives.

This is not an academic tome but a straightforward explanation of how children might feel and behave and the issues that might be involved. It offers practical advice and strategies to help you to help children confront and deal with troubled feelings. No one need be an expert in these matters – the reader does not need professional knowledge, but merely compassion and a desire to help.

Each person's grief and how they express it is individual to them. Other factors such as developmental stage, culture, belief, experience and nurture also come into the equation. When you read this, please take into account how you feel about a strategy or an approach and consider how suitable you feel it is for the child you are with.

Grief brings change. A grief resolved – that is, fully experienced and expressed – can be integrated into a person's life experience and help them treasure fond memories and move on. It can enable that person to have an increased understanding and compassion for others and take life as it is, with all its sorrows and joys.

Finally, nobody is perfect and we can only do our best. Just open your heart to your child, and show that you care and are alongside them at this difficult time.

CHAPTER 1

Talking with children when someone dies

Give sorrow words –
The grief that does not speak
whispers the o'er fraught heart,
and bids it break.

Macbeth, William Shakespeare

Accepting a child as a bereaved person

The most important point for adults to realise is that children do grieve, whatever their age. Some adults may recognise this but believe that they are 'protecting' them by not discussing such a powerful topic.

Adults who set out to protect children from the realities of death may:

- not talk about the death;
- not show any emotion in front of the child;
- pretend that all is normal;
- make sure that the child is not present at or involved in any ritual.

'When my grandfather died I was only five and remember being told to go and play in the garden. I sat on my swing thinking about my grandfather, feeling that I mustn't cry and wondering why I was excluded from all the support that was going on indoors with the adults.'
(Adult dealing with unresolved grief)

This kind of behaviour confuses children and is very likely to make them feel excluded. Even years after a death, adults can feel angry about being excluded:

- 'Why was I sent to my friend's house when my mum died and had her funeral? I never had time to say goodbye.'
- 'If I had known that my sister was so ill, I would have wanted to go and see her more.'

Children will pick up on what is not being said or done, and will take their cue from the adults around them.

Children who feel excluded from a family bereavement may:

- not cry in front of the family;
- bottle up feelings;
- feel unable to ask pertinent questions;
- feel excluded and confused;
- imagine far worse things.

Guy Perkins' poem, 'Small Talk' on page 11 deals with this issue very effectively. He describes normal events happening around a grieving child who wants to be able to talk about his or her grief.

> 'It helps to know why someone in the family is sad or worried. If you don't know, then you think that you're to blame or that it is worse than you thought. I felt so alone when my grandma died as no one spoke about it to me. Conversation stopped when I went into a room and no one talked to me about it or asked me how I felt.' *(Girl, aged 12)*

Describing grief as like an elephant in the room, which everyone is aware of but is trying to ignore, has become a common image since the publication of Terry Kettering's poem 'Elephant in the Room'.

Children who grieve alone or who bottle up feelings when someone significant to them dies will almost certainly have to deal with unresolved grief at a later time. Adults need to realise that children will naturally be upset, will need to be allowed to grieve and helped to express and deal with it, and must be part of the bereavement process.

Small Talk

Your knock wakes me and Tabby,
You give us both a pat.
The telly's on for breakfast,
The cat sits on the mat.
This horrid thing inside me
Is growing awfully fat.
You never say her name now
And all I hear is chat.
Small talk.

My friends at school are wary,
My teachers cut me slack.
They don't know what to say,
So I sit right at the back.
The thing inside weighs heavy
With questions I can't ask.
I walk around the playground
Voices shouting at my mask.
Small talk.

This ache inside my stomach
Is tearing me apart.
This monster of unknowing
Lies clamped around my heart.
Oh PLEASE just let me ask you,
I know you're also sore.
You raise your head, it's time for bed,
You squeeze a smile and feed me more –
Small talk.

Guy Perkins

Breaking the news

Who?

Breaking the news of a death in the family should preferably be carried out by the adult or adults who are emotionally closest to the child. However, it is possible that in some situations this person is so grief stricken that some other close relative or friend may be the right person to talk to the child.

Where?

If possible, take the child to a quiet place where you will be undisturbed and comfortable. Sit yourself and the child down before you speak.

How?

- Make sure you are as composed as possible and that you have the child's full attention. The exact words you use will depend on the stage of development of the child, the circumstances of the death and your relationship with the child, but start by saying you have some sad news you must tell them.

- Be as honest and open as possible and try not to use euphemisms – 'gone to sleep', 'passed away', 'lost' – that may confuse the child. Be direct and say that the person has died/is dying.

- Allow time and be prepared for a variety of reactions. If you have the opportunity, convey to the child that there is no set or 'correct' way to react.

- Children may be shocked or show disbelief. They may cry or be full of despair. Some may be quiet and stunned. Others may show what might seem inappropriate reactions, such as saying 'What are we having for tea?' and continuing with their usual activities. Usually children will ask questions, either straight away or on another occasion.

- Let them know that you care and are concerned about what has happened. Say that you want to help and be there for them if they want to talk more or ask more questions at a later time.

- Shedding tears yourself is normal, and shows the child how much the person meant to you.

Important things to say to bereaved children

Even if they don't express them initially, children of all ages will have fundamental worries and concerns that you will need to reassure them about straight away.

- Let them know who will take care of them, who will keep them safe.

- Tell them that there was nothing anyone could have done to change the outcome. Tell them that what has happened is nobody's fault.

- Tell them that the dead person did not choose to leave the child and that they cannot return.

- Let them know that everyone has different feelings and reactions, and that no one has the right to tell them what they feel or how they should feel.

- Emphasise that it will take some time to adjust and that sad feelings will come and go.

- Give assurance that you are there to share sadness, memories and questions, and say that maybe you can comfort each other.

'I thought for years that my baby sister died because I had accidentally banged her head one day.'

'I used to worry that my dad was killed because I had wished him dead when he told me off that morning.'

Well-meaning explanations that can confuse children

It is very easy for an adult to say something with the best possible intentions that the child misinterprets, resulting in confusion, anxiety or even resentment. Avoid using both euphemisms and blunt statements with no explanations.

Children's questions

After being told about a death, a child might ask questions straight away, maybe about how and when the person died. Having had time to think, other questions will emerge and be asked, if they feel comfortable enough to approach a caring adult, though not always at the most appropriate time or place!

The questions will obviously depend on the child's age and ability, but there is some commonality about the kinds of questions asked.

Immediate questions

- What do I do now?
- Who else knows?
- Who can I talk to?
- What do I say to other members of the family who are upset?

Practical questions

- Who will take care of me?
- Will I have to take care of the younger children?
- Who will take me to school/pick me up from football/make my lunch?
- Who is going to tell my teacher?
- What do I do about/say to my friends?

Questions relating to a child's fears

- Am I going to die too?
- Will I inherit the disease?
- Does dying hurt?
- Did I wish him/her dead?
- What did he/she do wrong?
- Is it my fault?
- How long will I live?
- Is he/she looking down on me?
- Will he/she become a ghost?

The need for information

- What does being dead mean?
- What is it like to die?
- How did he/she die?
- What do dead people look like?
- Why couldn't the doctor/hospital save her/him?
- Where has he/she gone?
- Is it okay to talk about it/cry/be normal?

Questions about the body and the funeral

- What happens at funerals?
- Where is the body?
- Can I see the body?
- What do they do with the body?
- How can I say goodbye/be involved?
- What happens to a dead person's body?

Answering children's questions

It is vital that adults treat children's questions seriously and openly. If it is not possible to answer straight away, then do explain this to the child and ensure that making a time to talk is given top priority.

What to remember

- Children need clear explanations. Admitting honestly that you don't know is better than giving elaborate answers you don't believe yourself.
- Avoid using euphemisms.
- If you give religious answers, make sure that you believe what you are saying and start by saying 'I believe...' or 'Some people believe...'. Make sure that your answers won't conflict with the religious upbringing of the child.
- Do not tell children half-truths. You could lose their trust and they will feel let down even many years later.
- Children take in as much as they can manage in one session. Don't give them too much information at one time.
- Children need to feel that talking about the death is an open subject and that they can express their thoughts and questions as they arise.

'When I was little, I came home and couldn't find my two tortoises. When I asked my parents if they had seen them they answered that the pair had 'gone away'. I felt so sad that they didn't like me or my garden. It wasn't until years later that I found out that the tortoises had been in the bonfire when my father lit it and my parents had lied to me so that I wouldn't be so upset. I felt very let down but relieved that my tortoises hadn't left my garden because they were unhappy. Yes, I would have been upset but I would have got over it. As it was, I lost some trust in my parents.'

Explaining death to children

Children develop a concept of death at a very early age, often at around four years. A child may already have mourned a pet or know people who have died or who have had a bereavement. They will have seen dead or dying insects, birds and plants around them, maybe animals run down by traffic. They may have some understanding of the cycle of seasons, how things blossom and grow in springtime and die away in autumn. The television and newspapers give reports of people dying in disasters or accidents and being murdered. Computer games, dramas, soap operas and the cinema tell stories of shooting, killing and death.

Explaining death to children will therefore have different starting points depending on their age and previous experience.

Do remember:

- that a good start could be to ask the child what they already know about death;

- to draw on what they have already experienced;

- that religious explanations about death are not appropriate unless the adult really believes in what he or she is saying – if a person believes then they can honestly say that they believe; if not, they might talk about what people of different religions believe;

- to ensure that whatever you say doesn't conflict with the religious upbringing of the child;

- to give explanations only if asked;

- to give only as much as the child can take in at one time; if they want to know more then they will ask another question.

What is death?

Death means that the person is not alive any more. They cannot talk, breathe, move, eat or do any of the things they did when they were living. Their body has stopped working.

If the dead person is elderly you might explain to a young child that their body just stopped working and the doctor couldn't fix it any more. The child might ask if they too are going to die, especially if the deceased is a young person. Explain that all living things will eventually die but that most people live until they are old and the child should expect to live a very long time.

Communicating sympathetically

The way adults communicate with children is so important. These contrasting examples show how children can be hindered or helped to work through their grief.

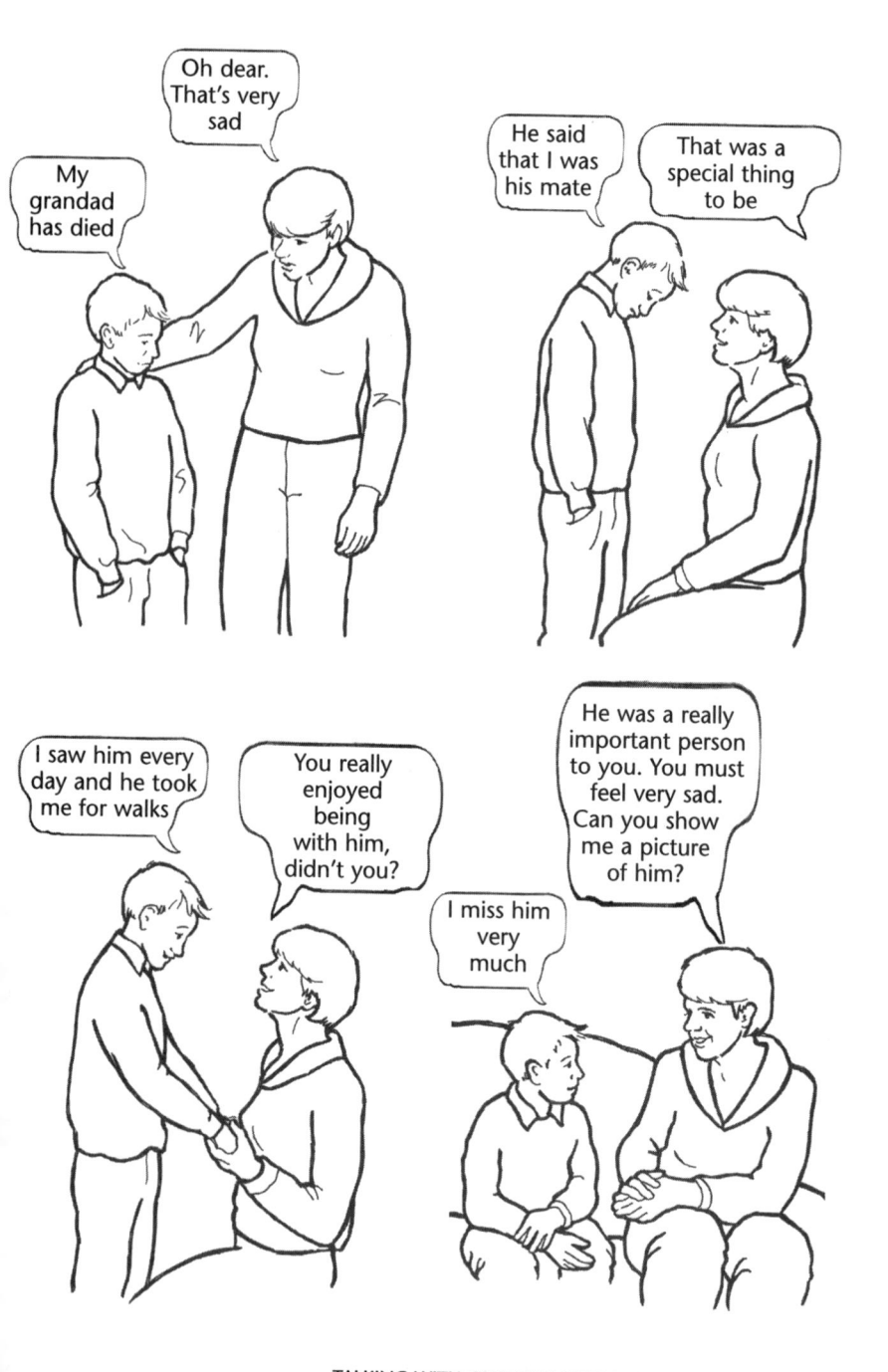

Lighting candles

Light a candle and talk about how it moves and flickers and gives off warmth and light. Then blow it out and ask the child whether the candle seems the same. Where has the movement and light gone? Explain that when someone dies the warmth and caring part of them called the spirit or soul leaves the body.

Using nature

If you are outside in the countryside or in a garden maybe you could talk about how everything in nature has a season – how plants and trees bud and blossom in the spring and die in the winter. The flowers and leaves die but the plant lives on in a different form. Nature has patterns – and plants, animals and people are part of that pattern.

Perhaps you could talk about the favourite tree or flower of the deceased and suggest that you plant something in their memory.

Relating to the death of a pet

If the child has experienced the death of a pet, they could be reminded of what happened then. You could talk about the good times they had with the pet and what happened when the pet died. They may remember what the pet looked like and how its body had stopped functioning. Maybe the child helped to bury the pet and gave it a 'funeral'.

Explaining accidents

If the person died as a result of an accident, you may have to explain what happened. Young children may have what might seem a morbid interest and want to know all the details about the death.

Telling stories

Telling a story might be helpful, and I give two examples here. The first, the analogy of the dragonfly, I remember being told in this context when I was a child. It has since been published as an illustrated story called *Waterbugs and Dragonflies* by Doris Stickney.

The waterbugs lived at the bottom of the pond and sometimes they looked up to the surface and wondered what was there. One day, one little waterbug felt that he just had to go and find out for himself so he climbed up and up a water reed until he left the water. Still he climbed, feeling the warm sunshine on his back. At the top of the reed, he rested and as he rested he felt his body changing. The old body was not important to him any more and he found that he could crawl out of it and leave it behind on the reed. He found that he had grown beautiful wings that gave a rainbow of colours in the sunshine. The sun warmed his wings and he realised that he could fly. Off he went enjoying the new world he found himself in. He settled on a waterlily and looked down into the water. He wonderered how his waterbug friends were and wanted to tell them about the new world he had discovered. He knew that his new body just couldn't go back into the water but also knew that one day his friends would join him when they too took the journey up the water reed.

This is an adaptation of the final part of *Watership Down*, which describes the rabbit's spirit leaving its body.

Hazel was in his burrow. He had spent a great deal of time there lately, for he felt the cold and could not seem to smell or run so well as in days gone by. He woke to realise that there was a rabbit lying quietly beside him.

'Do you want to talk to me?'

'Yes, that's what I've come for,' replied the other. 'You know me, don't you?'

'Yes, of course,' said Hazel. 'Yes, my Lord,' he said. 'Yes, I know you.'

'You've been feeling tired,' said the stranger, 'but I can do something about that. If you are ready, we might go along now.'

The sun was shining and in spite of the cold there were a few bucks and does at play. It seemed to Hazel that he would not be needing his body any more, so he left it lying on the edge of the ditch, but stopped for a moment to watch his rabbits.

'You need not worry about them,' said his companion. 'They'll be all right.'

He reached the top of the bank in a single, powerful leap. Hazel followed and together they slipped away, running easily down through the wood.

Using books and websites

There are many age-related fiction books that can be read to children or they can read for themselves. It is helpful for them to realise that what they are feeling and experiencing has been shared by others and that things do change and move on. Libraries and good bookshops will be able to assist in finding suitable books for the child.

A list of useful websites can be found on pages 93–94.

Summary

- Children experience grief and bereavement and are affected in many different ways.
- Grief is a process of several different stages and may continue for some time.
- Children who are excluded from sharing in the grief process are likely to have issues of unresolved grief in later life.
- Talk to children and answer their questions honestly, without using euphemisms.

The father came back from the funeral rites.
His boy of seven stood at the window, with
his eyes wide open and a golden amulet
hanging from his neck, full of thoughts
too difficult for his age.
His father took him in his arms and the
boy asked him: 'Where is mother?'
'In heaven,' answered his father, pointing
to the sky.
The boy raised his eyes to the sky and
long gazed in silence. His bewildered
mind sent abroad into the night the
question: 'Where is heaven?'
No answer came: and the stars seemed
like the burning tears of that ignorant
darkness.

Tagore, 1970

CHAPTER 2

How children might grieve

'Mum?' he whispered. 'Dad?'

They just looked at him, smiling. And slowly, Harry looked into the faces of the other people in the mirror and saw other pairs of green eyes like his, other noses like his, even a little old man who looked as though he had Harry's knobbly knees – Harry was looking at his family, for the first time in his life.

The Potters smiled and waved at Harry and he stared hungrily back at them, his hands pressed flat against the glass as though he was hoping to fall right through it and reach them. He had a powerful kind of ache inside him, half joy, half terrible sadness.

Harry Potter and the Philospher's Stone, J K Rowling, 1997

Grief is a process one goes through as a result of a bereavement. It is important to recognise that no two people are alike and neither is their grief. There are common features of the stages of grief but it does not mean that each individual will experience all of them or in a particular order:

Immediate grief

- shock – feeling numb;
- denial, disbelief;

Active grief

- searching and yearning;
- depression;
- despair;
- disorganisation;
- anger;
- guilt;
- bargaining;

Subsiding grief

- acceptance;
- healing;
- moving on.

Some people may get stuck at a particular stage and never progress from it.

There are various factors that influence children's grief (see page 33). Their perception mainly depends on their age, intellectual development and past experience.

Babies and children under five years

Babies will sense and be affected by the feelings of the adults around them and, as a result, may become restless and unhappy themselves.

Children at this stage have a limited understanding of the concept of death; younger children will not understand that death is final and tend to think in concrete terms.

This lack of understanding can explain the lack of reaction that children may show when learning of a death.

Toddlers can experience a loss of attachment to people close to them and have been known to try to search for them.

Children in this age group may also ask questions over and over again, which can be difficult and distressing for a grieving adult. It would not be unusual for children to regress to earlier behaviour like bedwetting or baby talk. They may become insecure and cling to a parent.

'Can we take Grandpa some food when we go to the cemetery?'

'Can we dig him up so that he can play with me?'

Matthew Bannister, who presents a Radio Four obituary programme, 'The Last Word', described the drowning of his wife. He was left with a 3-year-old daughter to console:

'I explained to her that Mummy had gone to Heaven and she seemed to take that on board and then said "Can we play?".'

'A voice for the departed', *The Times 2*, 31 January 2006

Five to nine years

Children in this age group will have gradually come to the understanding that all life functions end when a person is dead.

- They often show an almost morbid curiosity about death, rituals surrounding death and the functions of dead bodies. They may personalise death as monsters or ghosts. They might experience bad dreams and have sleeping difficulties.

- They still feel they are the centre of their universe so may feel guilty that they have caused the death because of being naughty or having bad thoughts about the dead person.

- They may have difficulties in expressing feelings and they may retreat inside themselves and become withdrawn or aggressive.

- They may demand reassurance and become insecure and anxious when adults leave them.

> 'When my father died, my little sister came with us to see his body. She shocked everyone by prodding him, and then she wanted to open his eyes.'
>
> *(Girl, aged 15)*

Nine to twelve years

Children in this age group are aware of the finality of death and recognise the possibility of their own death.

- They begin to grieve in a more adult way and may often deny the loss and try to get on with life. This could be exacerbated if adults around them say things like 'there's a brave girl' or 'big boys don't cry'.

- At this stage, children are often relating more to their peer group and the death of a parent may set them apart from friends and destabilise them.

- Children can become angry or aggressive without understanding why.

- Children may try to control the situation.

- Seeing friends who have all of their family may emphasise their loss.

Decca Aikenhead, whose mother died of breast cancer when she was 10, wrote in her article 'Things Left Unsaid' (*Guardian Weekend*, 29 October 2005) that she remembers straight after her mother's death playing games of forfeits in her head:

'What would I give in exchange for having my mother back? A year in prison? Five? One of my legs? I was cycling down the lane past the dairy one afternoon, happily absorbed in the game, when suddenly it hit me. There was no deal. I could offer what I liked, but she wasn't coming back.'

'I went to my friend's house and she fell over and hurt her knee. Her mum gave her a cuddle and put a plaster on. I was overwhelmed by the fact that my mother would never do that again.' (*Girl, aged 11*)

Adolescents

Adolescents are able to grieve as adults do. However, they have the added pressure of having to cope with all the physical and social changes that are also happening to them. It may often be hard to tell whether their conduct is an expression of grief or merely typical adolescent behaviour.

People are very sympathetic when a young person loses a parent and will often excuse bad behaviour or let them off pressures such as homework, going to school or helping around the house. This can, however, exacerbate young people's feelings of aloneness and adults would be kinder to provide a firm structure to preserve some order in their lives.

- Friends play an important part of the grieving process for the adolescent.

- Young people may search for meaning through religion and interest in the afterlife.

- They may try to evade grief by indulging in risk-taking behaviour such as misusing substances and alcohol abuse or look for comfort in risky sexual behaviour.

- They may become withdrawn, depressed, detached or, at worse, suicidal.

- They may have mood swings and create tension within the family.

- Some adolescents find themselves forced into an adult role and resent having to care for younger siblings or having more demanding domestic responsibilities.

Decca Aikenhead remembers that women would stop her in the village shop and say: 'Your mother was an angel.' This deification, rather than comforting her, made her lose the sense of what her mother actually was to her. For the next twenty years she tells of the role her dead mother played – one of a formidable ghostly rival. She went on to describe that as an adolescent she began to regard a dead mother as an extraordinary piece of good fortune as she studied her adolescent friends' problems with their mothers. Her experiences provide a wonderful insight into how children and young people may think, and how the bereavement process influences their adult emotional life.

Expressions of children's grief

The ways in which children experience grief vary and many of them are common to those of adults. However, other behaviour may not immediately be recognised as expressions of grief and can be cause for concern.

Mood swings
Eating for comfort or as an act of denial
Sleep disturbances
Withdrawal
Insecurity – reluctance to leave an adult's side
Regression to an earlier state of development
Physical and verbal aggression
Complaining of non-specific aches and pains
Susceptibility to coughs and colds – a low immune system
Risk-taking – a 'couldn't care less' attitude
Excessive worrying about their own and others' health and safety
Lack of concentration, especially at school
Reluctance to go to school
Lethargy – a lack of interest in activities or friends
Helplessness
Feelings of anger, guilt, fear and anxiety
Obsessive habits
Challenging behaviour
Experiencing symptoms of the illness of the deceased
Apathy
Stress-induced illnesses

If these signs persist, then the adults caring for the child should seek professional help. A good place to start would be discussions with parents, the school and the child's GP.

Factors that influence a child's grief

The way a child copes with grief, both immediately and in the long term, is affected by their circumstances and how the grief is dealt with at the time.

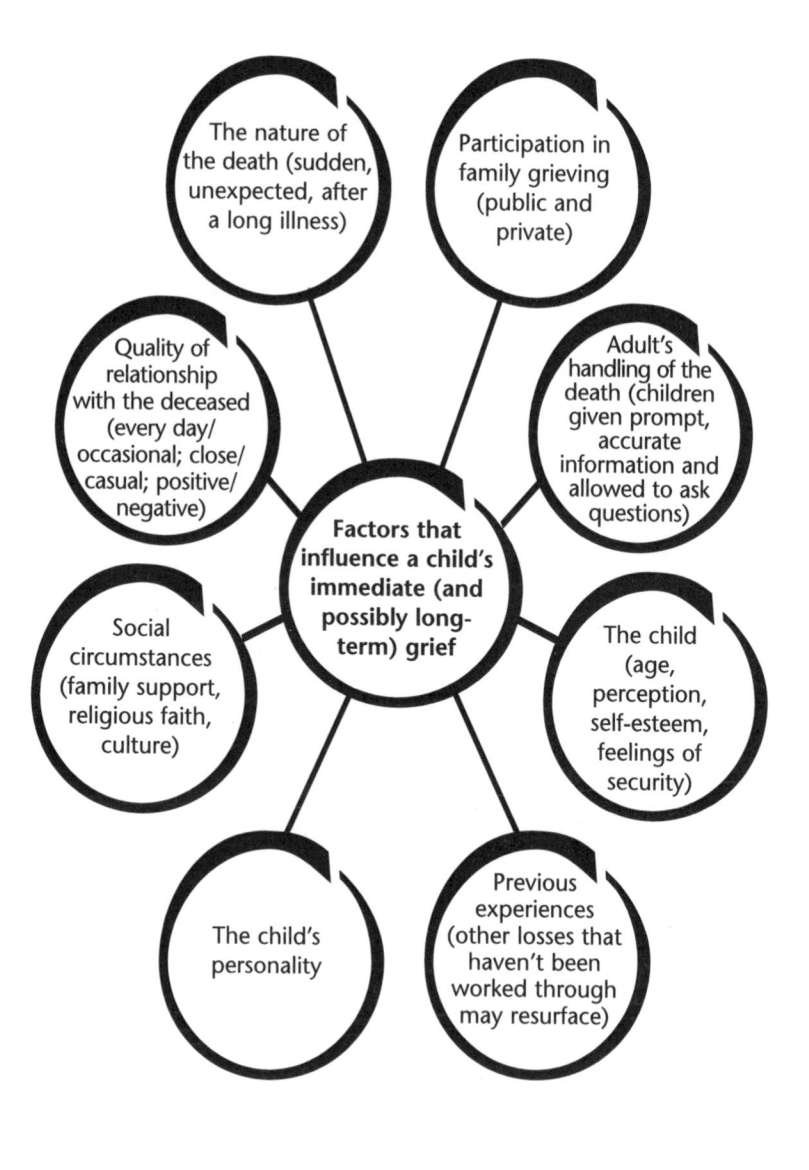

The nature of the death (sudden, unexpected, after a long illness)

Participation in family grieving (public and private)

Quality of relationship with the deceased (every day/ occasional; close/ casual; positive/ negative)

Adult's handling of the death (children given prompt, accurate information and allowed to ask questions)

Factors that influence a child's immediate (and possibly long-term) grief

Social circumstances (family support, religious faith, culture)

The child (age, perception, self-esteem, feelings of security)

The child's personality

Previous experiences (other losses that haven't been worked through may resurface)

Factors that determine a child's development after the death of a parent

The death of a parent will result in significant changes for a child and its family. Every child has its own personality and coping strategies, and every grief reaction will be different, even amongst brothers and sisters. There are, however, influences that will also affect the long-term grieving and healing process. There is no right or wrong way for a surviving parent to support their child but it is helpful if they consider the following possibilities that will affect the child's grief and healing.

Before the death
The family

- There may have been disruption to family life before the death – a parent may have been ill or the family might have been going through a difficult time.
- The family may have been very close and supportive.
- The child may have been used to having grandparents, extended family and friends close at hand who were part of everyday life and used to the family routine.
- The wider family may have been living at some distance, so this kind of support would not be available.

The child

- The kind of personality the child already had.
- The kind of relationships that the child already had with the parents and the rest of the family.
- The child's involvement in clubs and organisations that were already supportive.
- The child may have already acquired social and life skills that will help them to cope.
- The position of a child in the family may be significant; the eldest child will often act more responsibly and the baby of the family may be shielded from negative events.

Immediately after the death
The deceased parent

- The parent may have been ill for some time and the child may have been prepared for the death.

- The child may have had a special bond with the parent or may not have been very close.
- The child may have had the opportunity to say goodbye to the parent before or after the death.

Grief reactions

- The child will most likely take their cue from how the surviving parent and other adult relatives are grieving.
- How adults communicate to the child about the death.
- How the child is involved with the mourning process.
- Whether there is the support of other significant relationships.
- The child's age and development will affect how they react to the death.
- Girls and boys may react differently depending on how adults around them view emotional reactions of different genders.

It would be helpful for adults to consider how changes in circumstances and relationships can influence the child's healing process. They can then consider how to support a child through possible future developments in life.

Later
The surviving parent

- The surviving parent will have to cope with their own needs as well as coping with the children single-handed.
- There may be a loss of income or more financial strain for the cost of child care.
- If a parent is working hard to support the family, there may be reduced contact with the child.
- How the surviving parent helps him or herself and their children work through the experience of grieving.

Home

- The family set-up and routines will be different.
- There may be more chores or more responsibility for the child.
- The child may be cared for by siblings, or may have to care for them.
- There may be a house move.
- They may have to get used to living with less money.

The future
Changing relationships

- How the deceased parent is acknowledged and remembered will be important.
- The parent will eventually have to make a new social life.
- The parent may meet new friends and partner(s).
- The child will have to face the possibility of these new people becoming part of their life.

New families

- How a child copes with changes and new relationships.
- A child may have to live with the new partner and their children.
- A child will need to know how they can treasure their happy memories and then move on within the family set-up.

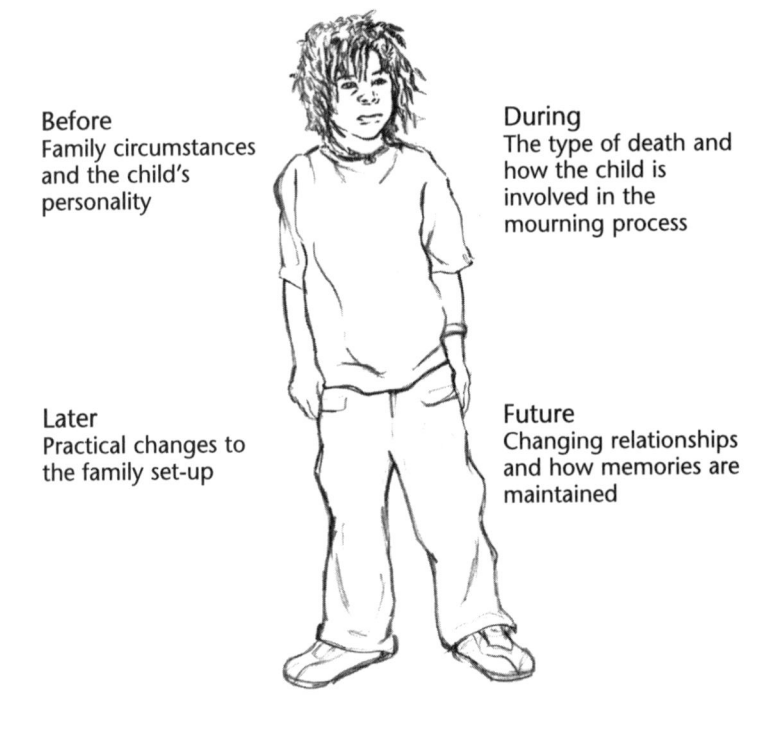

Before
Family circumstances and the child's personality

During
The type of death and how the child is involved in the mourning process

Later
Practical changes to the family set-up

Future
Changing relationships and how memories are maintained

Thinking about the particular influences on the child at different stages will help in the healing process.

Explosive reactions to loss and unresolved grief

Grieving children and adults will temporarily experience a whole spectrum of negative feelings. To avoid them becoming deep-rooted, try to practise the positive expressions of good grief (see page 38).

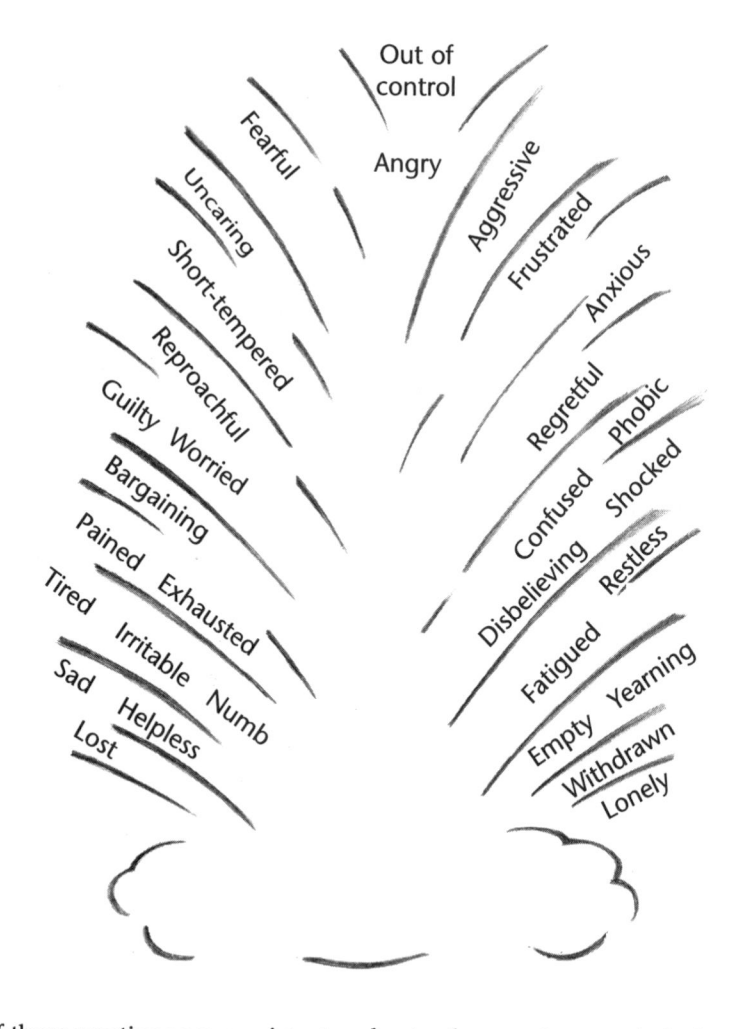

If these reactions are persistent and extend over a long period of time, then professional help needs to be sought. A good place to start would be discussions with the school, parents and the child's GP.

Positive expressions of grief

Given the opportunity to grieve well, a child's grief is more likely to be resolved. Children tend to grieve for a shorter time than adults, but if they have unresolved grief it will reappear at times of renewed grief or sadness. Adults must be reassured that they can't always be perfect and get it right, but here are some pointers towards grieving well.

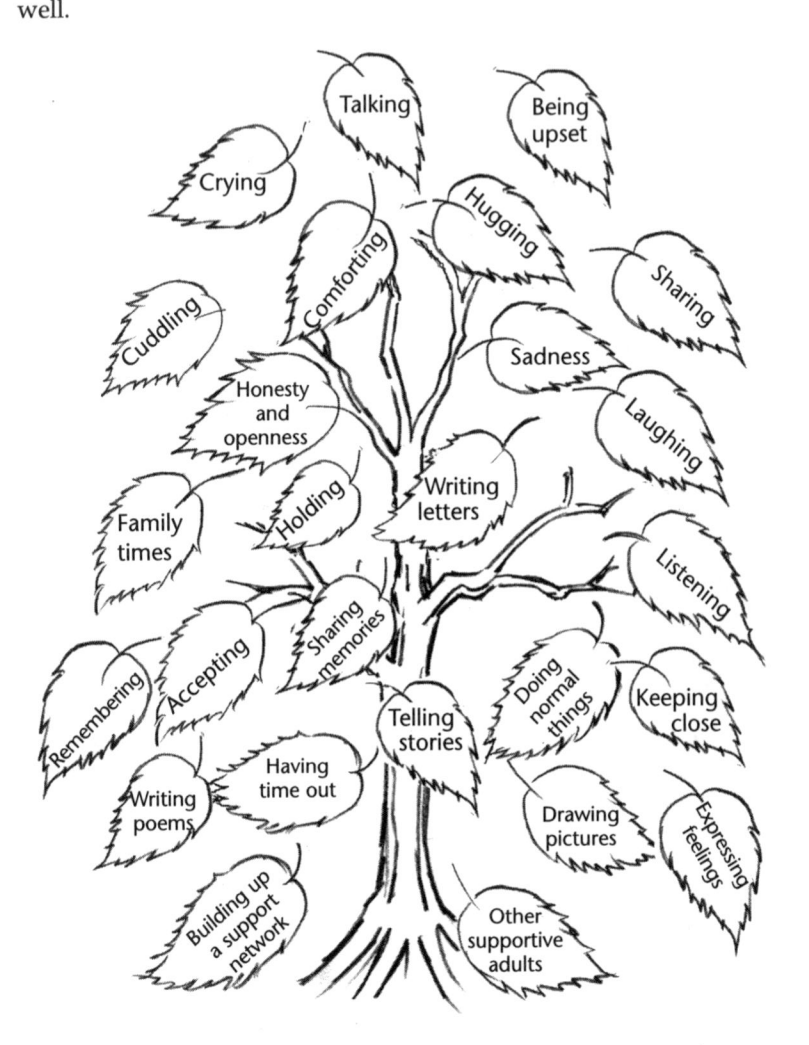

A grief resolved – one that is fully experienced and expressed – can be integrated into a person's life experience, help them treasure fond memories and help them move on.

Feelings

Children may feel overloaded with emotions during a bereavement. They need to know that this is natural and also that it is usual for feelings to come and go and change, maybe from cheerful to miserable very quickly. They may feel guilty if they are feeling happy and need to be reassured that it is okay to carry on with everyday life.

It is helpful for a child to be able to identify these strong feelings. It could be useful to sit down with the child daily to identify all the feelings they may be experiencing. By using the 'How Are You Feeling?' pictures below, even very young children can identify their emotions.

When they have done this, it is important not to ask for an explanation unless the child wants to tell you. If they are very sad, a hug or a touch on the arm might be the most appropriate thing. The adult might want to say: 'Would you like to talk about it?' The child needs to know that these feelings are natural, that there is someone there to talk to if that would help, and that talking can help strong feelings subside.

Some children may wish to make a chart of their feelings, or draw how they are feeling, or complete a wall of feelings (see page 41). Older children may prefer to do this exercise on their own.

How are you feeling?

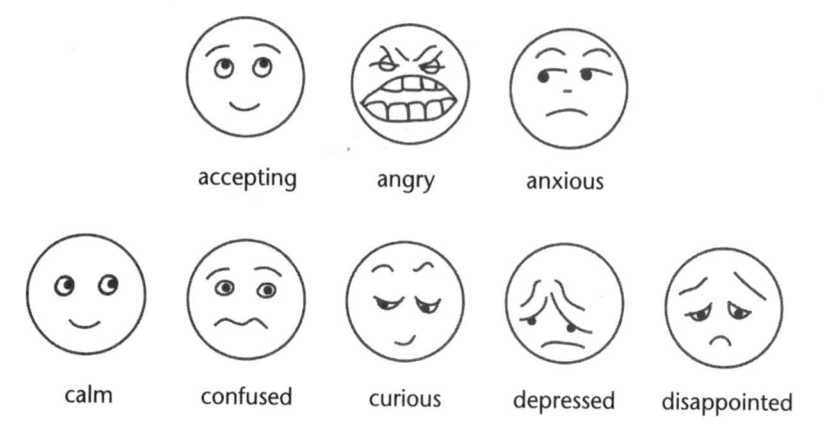

accepting   angry   anxious

calm   confused   curious   depressed   disappointed

How are you feeling?

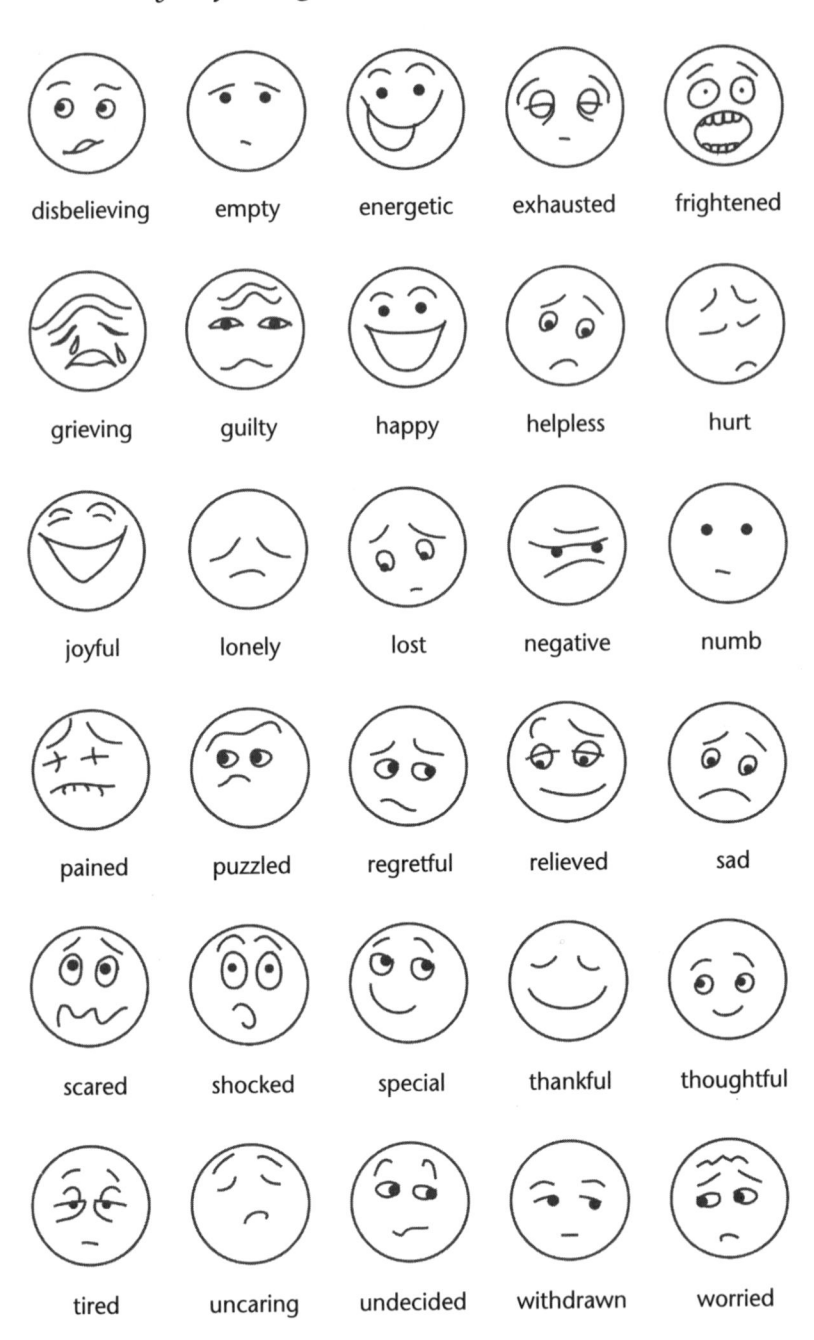

disbelieving · empty · energetic · exhausted · frightened

grieving · guilty · happy · helpless · hurt

joyful · lonely · lost · negative · numb

pained · puzzled · regretful · relieved · sad

scared · shocked · special · thankful · thoughtful

tired · uncaring · undecided · withdrawn · worried

The wall of feelings

Some children may find it helpful to fill in a wall of feelings like this one, which helps them to identify their emotions.

What grieving children need

Children need to know that they have at least one adult they can rely on, someone who can help them with the following:

- information on what has happened and why;
- information on what will happen next;
- reassurance that they will be cared for and are not to blame;
- asking questions, and having them answered as honestly and openly as possible;
- being involved in the grieving process as much as they want to;
- expressing their feelings;
- talking freely about the deceased;
- having a support network;
- reassurance that their world has not completely disintegrated;
- being with adults who also share their feelings and who will allow children to offer them comfort and support.

What adults can do to help

Adults must acknowledge their responsibility to support the children in their care who are affected by grief. This checklist offers some useful ideas:

- Acknowledge children's grief and understand some of the key issues of childhood grief.

- Answer children's questions as openly and honestly as possible and do not be afraid of saying 'I don't know'.

- Include children in the mourning process as much as possible and help them to say goodbye in a way that is meaningful for them.

- Keep the memory of the dead person alive and real; talk about him or her and encourage the child to remember and have access to photographs.

- Treat children as normally as possible but anticipate possible negative behaviour patterns.

- Try to keep day-to-day normality going.

- Remember that the grieving process is a journey, not an event; children will revisit questions, issues and feelings.

- Do grief work with the child (see chapter 5).

- Remember that a child's period of intense grieving can be a lot shorter than that of adults but the grieving process lasts much longer, sometimes into adulthood.

The bereaved adult

As well as supporting and comforting the child, a bereaved adult will be trying to cope with their own grief, as well as practical issues arising from the death. It is vitally important that the adult considers his or her own well-being.

- Involve other helpful people in your care for your child – build a network of support for yourself and your child.

- Be kind and gentle with yourself.

Summary

- No two people are alike and neither is their grief.
- Children's reactions to death change as they develop.
- Various factors such as family support, religious faith and culture will influence a child's reaction to grief.
- Grieving children need to be involved in the grieving process.

No one ever told me that grief felt so like fear.
I am not afraid, but the sensation is like being afraid.
The same fluttering in the stomach,
the same restlessness, the yearning.

C S Lewis

CHAPTER 3

Rituals around death: the importance of saying goodbye

Worn out clothes are cast off by the body.
Worn out bodies are cast off by the person who lives in them.

From the Hindu Gita

Involving children in rituals around death

From the beginning of time, people have tried to make sense of death and have developed many rituals to celebrate a dead person's life, say farewell and prepare the body for the afterlife.

In the past, children would often have been an integral part of this process, but in recent history death seems to have become more removed and separate. Children's involvement in rituals also varies depending on their family's culture and religious views.

The function of death rituals is to:

- celebrate the person's life;
- gather people together formally to show support and respect;
- help make the unreal real;
- give and receive comfort and assurance;
- provide the opportunity to grieve formally/ritually;
- symbolise the transition from life to death;
- bring structure and order to a chaotic situation;
- give the opportunity for people outside the family to pay their respects;
- follow religious beliefs and practices;
- say a final goodbye.

Some adults may be quite reluctant to allow children to be involved in any part of this. They may exclude children because they are overwhelmed by their own grief and feel that they can't bear to see the children unhappy or don't want to give the children any further distress.

Children have just as great a need as adults to have a structure for their grief – to make real the unreal situation they find themselves in. Being part of the funeral ceremony or other death rituals can help children to understand and come to terms with their grief. The alternative may be that their imaginations run riot with worries, misconceptions and fears; what they don't see may be scarier than what they do. If they are not given the choice to take part they may regret later on not having had the opportunity to say that final goodbye. They might grieve the lack of closure for many years afterwards.

Children should either be:

- given the choice of joining in with the grown ups;
- or sensitively and appropriately informed about all that took place if they were not present, and helped to create rituals of their own.

Seeing the body

Despite these familiar statements, children should be allowed to make up their own minds about whether or not they see the body of the deceased. It may reinforce the 'deadness' for them and help them to realise that burial and cremation is only for the body and not the real

'Let them remember her as she was.'

'The children are too young, they'll get upset.'

'You don't want to see your daddy now he's dead, do you?'

essence of the dead person. It will help them to say their final goodbye and will save them imagining dreadful things.

In order for them to make a proper decision they will have to be told what to expect. For example:

Daddy's body is at the funeral directors' chapel of rest. It is a small room with a high window showing the branches of a tree in the garden. There is no one else in the room and the only movement is a lit candle near the coffin, which is on a small table with the lid open.

Daddy is lying in the coffin with his head on a satin pillow. He is wearing his best suit – the one he wore to Auntie Margaret's wedding and he looks very peaceful with his eyes closed. His body isn't like it used to be – he isn't breathing any more, he can't walk, talk, eat or sleep. His skin looks whiter than usual and he feels quite cold. His body is all that is left for us to see but his spirit and our memories of him live on.

If you want to, you can put a little gift in the coffin or one of your drawings. If you don't want to come then I can do that for you.

Would you like to go and see the body?

Bear in mind that the child may change his or her mind, perhaps several times, and give them the opportunity to do so. They may need to have time to think of what they would like to say or take with them. If they want to leave a gift in the coffin, they may need help in deciding what would be most appropriate. Allow time for them to ask more questions so that they are well prepared.

The visit

Young children will probably be matter-of-fact about this visit. They might need to be lifted up to see and will most likely be full of questions. This might be quite disconcerting to adults present unless they realise the child's particular stage and perceptions. If the child is bringing a gift, he or she might insist on having it positioned in a particular way. They may appear disrespectful by poking the body to see if they can get a response and to check out what 'dead' means. Others will be very quiet, taking it all in. Older children may ask to have private time alone with the body. If there is more than one child – and especially if there is a significant age difference – it might be best to give each child the opportunity to visit at separate times.

- Try not to speak too much so that the child can take in everything or ask questions or just be silent and reflective.
- Let them know that they can touch or kiss the body – they might feel that they are not allowed.
- You can invite them to say something in the form of a goodbye. Young children may need only a few minutes before coming out, leaving the adults to spend their own special time alone with the body.

Funerals

Although children must never be forced into attending a funeral, they should be given the choice. They might change their mind a few times so, again, it is important for the adult to allow time and to explain what is likely to take place:

We are having a special ceremony for Daddy called a funeral at the mosque/synagogue/church/crematorium.

Lots of people will be there to say goodbye. All the rest of the family are coming from Dorset, except your little cousins. I expect that they too will be feeling very sad and some people might be upset and cry – but that is okay.

Daddy's coffin will be at the funeral with the lid down. It will be placed right in the centre for everyone to see and we have arranged to have some lovely flowers put on top.

At the funeral some people will stand up and talk about Daddy and do some readings. We have also chosen some songs that he liked.

After the service Daddy's body will be taken to the cemetery/ crematorium and will be buried/burned. We will then all come home and have something to eat and drink and will be able to talk to everybody.

The adult can then ask the child if he or she wants to go to the funeral, though offering an alternative if the child would prefer not:

Would you like to come to the service?

Would you like to come to the burial/crematorium?

Would you like to stay with Auntie Margaret and then come and join us at the party afterwards?

Would you like to make up our own goodbye service for Daddy?

If the child doesn't attend then maybe someone could spend some time with him/her as soon as they return and tell them what went on. They could bring a few flowers back as a keepsake or take the child to the graveside or the crematorium soon after. It might be more appropriate to work with the child to create a special ceremony of their own.

Children may find that being part of a more personal, child-friendly ceremony would be more relevant and private. However, they could have the choice of attending the formal funeral and then having a ceremony of their own.

Some ideas are:

- Planning their own service with readings, songs and prayers. Deciding where and when it will take place and what they will use – photographs, candles and music, for example.
- Writing letters, making drawings and then having a ceremony round a small fire in the garden where they place their offerings and watch the smoke rise up.
- Lighting a candle at a special time every day where the family can gather and say prayers or talk about a special memory. This can be very helpful in the early days – but be careful that it doesn't become a ritual that the family then becomes 'stuck' in and that prevents them moving on.
- Making up a ceremony for planting a tree in the garden and burying some letters, poems or drawings at the roots.
- Sending off balloons into the sky after a ceremony of prayers and readings.

Different customs and traditions

Taking part in funerals and rituals will also depend on the child's family customs, culture, beliefs and traditions. Adults who are working with grieving children not in their own family will need to know a little about what the child may be experiencing at home.

If the coffin is open and at home, children will obviously be more involved. If relatives and friends are visiting the house with food, saying prayers and sharing meals then again the children of the house will naturally be involved.

British culture regarding death has become rather sanitised. The body is taken away by the undertakers who do most of the arrangements, often with a minister who does not know the dead person. The wake (or funeral get-together) has become a buffet in a nearby hotel so that people can get back to their homes and work. For practising Christians, however, there is more detail, organisation, and support, depending on their beliefs and customs.

Most religions that originate in the East tend to want to bury or cremate their dead quickly because in hot countries bodies decay rapidly. However, in Britain the funeral cannot take place until after a death certificate has been issued; in any case, family members will need time to arrange travel to get to the funeral.

People of other religions living in Britain are also finding that their way of saying goodbye is changing and that many of their traditional practices are being lost or modified.

The following descriptions are very broad and general. Within each tradition and culture there is a range of diversity, depending on where the family originates in the world, what is available and whether the family is orthodox, traditional or has a modern approach.

Burial or cremation

Many orthodox Christians, Muslims and Jews believe that the dead will come back to life to be with God. They therefore choose to be buried rather than cremated. However, other Christians, Muslims and Jews now prefer cremation. Hindu children are often buried.

Buddhists, Hindus and Sikhs traditionally cremate their dead.

Buddhism

Buddhists believe in reincarnation, so tend to view death as a natural cycle of life. If the dead person has lived a truly unselfish life then they will reach Nirvana – bliss.

The body is ceremonially washed by members of the same gender and placed in an open coffin. Family and friends gather round to chant prayers and there is incense and ceremonial food.

Funerals tend to be joyful occasions and those attending will have the opportunity to ponder on the quality of their own lives. Buddhists recite their most important prayer – 'The Three Jewels', concerning Buddha, the Dharma (Buddha's way of life) and Snagha (the way for Buddhist monks). The 'Five Precepts' (the rules for living a good life) are also recited, so that all present can reflect on how they should be conducting the rest of their lives.

The body is normally cremated and the remains buried. The prayers continue for seven weeks after the death and are then repeated on every anniversary of the death.

Christianity

Christians believe in eternal life through the resurrection of Jesus Christ. Death is not something to be feared but should be anticipated with the hope of being united with God in heaven.

The body is normally washed, dressed and laid in a coffin at the chapel of rest, usually by an undertaker.

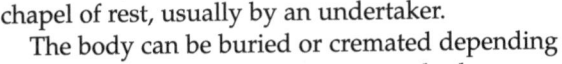

The body can be buried or cremated depending on personal choice, although more orthodox Christians will choose burial. There is often a memorial service a short time after the funeral.

Roman Catholics and some Anglicans have the Last Rites said at the bedside by the priest as the person is dying or before the body is moved. Often the coffin is laid in the church overnight before the funeral. The funeral will probably include the Mass (the taking of bread and wine) and sprinkling of holy water.

West Indian Christian funerals are much grander occasions, with a long service where members of the family sing and speak. The lid of the coffin is often open during the service and people may file past it and greet the family gathered by the coffin. In a West Indian home, people will be coming and going most of the time and the coffin may be laid open in one of the rooms. Family and friends often carry the coffin to the graveside for the committal. Members of the family pick up shovels and fill in the grave while others sing.

Hinduism

Hindus believe in reincarnation and, if a person has lived a good life, then in the next life they will be happier and in a better social position. The people at the top of this hierarchy are the Brahmins and they are more likely to return to Brahman (the universal soul) and happiness for eternity.

The body is ritually washed (if possible with water from the Ganges river) by members of the same gender. The eyes are closed, the limbs straightened and jewellery, sacred threads and other religious objects are left on or near the body. The body is left at the home or brought to the house just before the funeral. There will be an offering of pinda (rice balls and milk) for the dead person at a shrine every day for ten days. Relatives and friends traditionally come on the fourth and eleventh days to offer pinda and share in the family's grief.

Family members will carry the coffin into the house, taking off their shoes at the door. The floor of the room may be covered in a white sheet and the room will have incense burning and pictures of the dead person and Hindu gods. Friends and family will gather round to chant and scatter flower petals.

Just before the coffin is taken out of the house, the lid will be screwed down with the help of the eldest surviving son, even if he is a child (in India, the eldest son would light the fire on the pyre, so this practice has been adapted for the West).

There will probably be another service at the crematorium, with the eldest son taking a lead. Women usually stay behind at the house. Four to five males will be selected to witness the coffin going into the cremator to be burned. It is believed that the spirit leaves the body at this moment. Finally, the priest stands with a picture of a Hindu god and everyone files past and bows and prays to the god, and places money in a bowl.

Friends will visit several times a day for the first week and relatives may stay at the house.

Humanism

Humanists do not believe in any god or afterlife. They believe that death is the end of the person and is natural and inevitable. However, there are Humanist celebrants who can work with the family to provide a non-religious ceremony to celebrate the life of the deceased and to say farewell in a meaningful way.

The style of the funeral will be of the family's choice.

Islam

Death is part of Allah's will and plan of life for a Muslim. There will be a day of judgement on which records of the individual's actions will lead them to paradise or hell.

The body is ritually washed by members of the same gender. Non-Muslims are required to wear gloves when handling the body. The eyes are closed, the limbs straightened, the feet tied together and thread is tied around the toes. The face is bandaged to keep the mouth and eyes closed and the head is turned towards the right shoulder to face Mecca. The body is then wrapped in a sheet, which is knotted at the end.

Muslims try to bury their dead as soon after the death as possible. Friends and family will carry the coffin and family members will fill in the grave themselves.

After a death, the family mourners do not cook for themselves for 40 days but receive food from relatives, friends and neighbours, who will also gather to share memories of the dead person. At the end of the 40 days, the family invites all of the relatives and friends for a meal, which consists of the dead person's seven favourite foods.

Judaism

Jews believe that death is part of life, which will continue in heaven after death.

There is often a deathbed confession and prayers and readings as the person is dying. After death, the eyes and mouth are closed, the arms are place parallel with the hands unclenched and the legs straightened. The body is ceremonially washed by people of the same gender and covered with a white sheet.

Jews usually bury their dead, though some reform Jews are cremated. They try to have the funeral as soon as possible after the death.

For the first week, the closest relatives to the dead person do not eat meat or drink wine and they sometimes restrict activities such as listening to music. For the first month after a death, some Jews will not cut their hair, shave or wear new clothes.

Sikhism

Sikhs believe in a cycle of reincarnation leading to a merging of the soul with God. After a person dies their soul passes into another body (transmigration); the body is therefore cremated as the soul has no more use for it.

The body is ceremonially washed by people of the same gender, the eyes and mouth are closed, the limbs straightened and the body is wrapped in a white sheet. If baptised, the traditional Sikh symbols will be worn: Kesh (uncut hair), Kandha (wooden comb), Kara (steel bracelet), Kachera (cotton undershorts) and Kirpah (symbolic sword).

The funeral and cremation will be similar to that of a Hindu, taking place as soon as possible after the death. The ashes will be scattered on a river or in the sea.

After the funeral, gifts of food and money will be given to charity and everyone shares in a meal to remind each other that life must go on.

Summary

- Children should be involved in the process of saying goodbye.
- Children might find being involved easier than being excluded and shielded – their imagination may be worse than what is actually happening.
- Children should be prepared by being told exactly what to expect when seeing the body or attending the funeral or any other ritual or ceremony.
- It is helpful for adults working with bereaved children to have some idea of what the child may be experiencing within the family as part of the death process.

CHAPTER 4

Grieving children and their community

When, in the wake of nature's wrath, communities try to put together again some semblance of a normal life, it is suddenly and painfully obvious which pieces of the jigsaw are missing.

Nothing can tell a sharper tale of tragedy than empty hat-pegs in a school cloakroom.

The Namashal Vidyalayam School in Galle, southern Sri Lanka, is only one among many to have been hurt to its core. Of its 313 pupils, 150 are known to have died and 11 are still missing.

Across Sweden, where children return to school today, candles will be lit on the desks of as many as 100 children believed to have died in the tsunami, and their classmates will remember them in silence before discussing the tragedy.

There are at least four empty hat-pegs in British schools too.

Report on the tsunami, *The Times*, 11 January 2005

Adults in contact with the bereaved child – extended family, family friends and neighbours

During and after a death, practical and emotional support to a family has great benefits to the child. Parents may be very occupied with their own grief and the organisation and responsibilities that a death brings. They will most likely appreciate offers of domestic help and child care.

Adults who are caring for a grieving child might remember the following points and find them helpful:

- When the child comes to your home or when you take them out, they may just want to enjoy the normality and refuge of everyday living to escape for a while from the grief that is surrounding them at home.

- Listen to the child for cues as to whether they want to talk about their feelings or not.

- Listen to the child if they talk about their feelings or the deceased and prompt only gently – don't take over the conversation.

- Comfort the child if he or she talks about the deceased and becomes upset, but don't try to distract them or try to 'make things better'; remember that it may be your discomfort that makes talking about death a taboo, not the child's.

- It is good for the child to be able to express and show feelings.

- Try not to ask leading questions that might influence a child's decisions or to deflect the child from whatever emotion he or she is going through.

> 'Why don't you stay with me when they all go to the funeral?'
>
> 'I would rather have a burial than be burned.'
>
> 'Don't cry, dry your eyes, and let's go and find something to do.'

- Avoid giving opinions or judgements or making statements that would go against the wishes and needs of the immediate family.

- Be careful what you say when speaking to other adults with the child within earshot.

- When you talk about the deceased, do so naturally and spontaneously; don't try to put them on a pedestal and make them 'angels' – angels are hard to live up to and compensate for.

- A child's mood may easily change – don't be surprised if he or she needs more attention than usual.

> 'When my grandma died, I was very puzzled that none of the adults seemed upset. At the funeral, one of my aunties started to cry and that made me feel better as I could see that she cared for her mum. However, my uncle told her off and told her to pull herself together.'
>
> *(Boy, 16)*

- You don't have to be brave in front of the child if you feel sad or like crying; just explain that you too are very sad, which will show the child that you have feelings and that you care.

Returning a child to the community after a death

Parents should be prepared to help a child reintegrate into school and the wider community after a death.

- Work with the school to prepare for the child going back to school. See opposite for a sample letter to the school.
- Invite some close friends of the child round to the house so that the child begins by seeing a few children at a time.
- When the child returns to school, arrange for a few close friends to be there to greet him or her and give support throughout the day.
- Accept offers of help from neighbours, family and friends to care for your child.
- Reassure your child by ensuring that they know where you are and how you can be contacted when you are not together.
- Be open and honest with your child – ask how they got on with school and other activities, ask about feelings and share your own ups and downs.

Sample letter to school

8 Horsefield Gardens
Watermead
Slough
Berkshire

Dear Mrs Smith

As you will know, Jenny's mother died unexpectedly last week and Jenny has been at home with us.

It has been a traumatic time for all of us and I am concerned that Jenny receives as much support as she possibly can from the adults and children that she comes into contact with.

I have tried to be open and honest with Jenny and answer her questions as best I can. She seems to be coping with it all rather well but is, however, reluctant to return to school.

I would be grateful if we could meet as soon as possible to discuss how we can jointly help Jenny to reintegrate back into school and be supported over the next few months.

Yours sincerely

Thomas Berry

Caring for children who work and play with a bereaved child

Schoolmates, friends, cousins and neighbours who work and play with a grieving child may need help themselves in supporting their friend. Very young children are just accepting but the older they get the more sensitive they become to what is happening and may feel awkward about being with a sad playmate. They will, however, play an important part in normalising a child after a bereavement.

Bearing in mind the differing ages of the children, adults who care for them could try the following approaches:

- Encourage them to make cards and drawings to express their concern and friendship. Help them by suggesting what they could put: 'Eric, I am so sorry to hear about your sister. I know that you will miss her very much and must be feeling sad. Can I help you with your paper round this week? Do ring me and come round if you would like some company.'

- Children looking on may feel a sense of helplessness. Think of pleasant things children could do with the child, such as sleepovers, watching a video and going to the park to play football.

- Answer children's questions about death and dying if they arise, following the guidance in this book.

Help these children by:

- Explaining that their friendship will be an important source of support. Everyday social activities that they normally do will offer a much-needed distraction and give the grieving child a sense of normality.
- Telling them that they might see some change in their friend's behaviour: they might be withdrawn or seem very angry or sad; they might want to talk about what happened or might want to ignore it all.
- Telling them that if they are worried about their friend or if their friend tells them something that concerns them to pass it on to a caring adult.

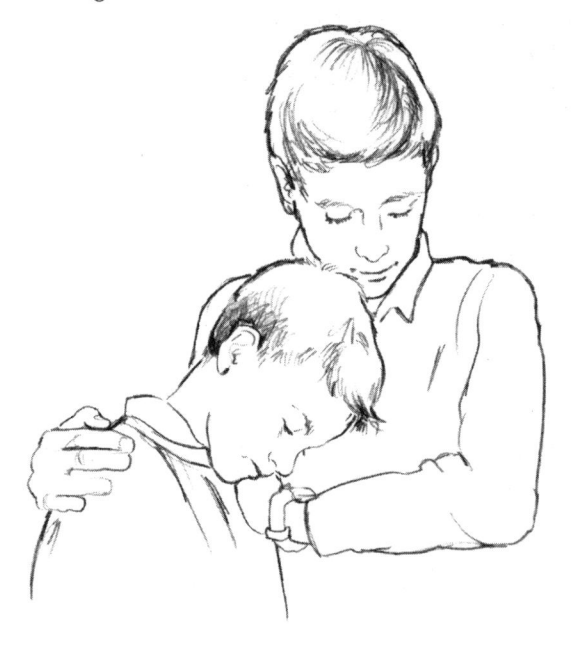

Be aware that:

- Seeing a friend's grief, children may develop fears about losing their own loved ones.
- For children who have already experienced a bereavement, observing this new experience may bring back painful memories.
- The children close to the grieving child may need extra help from you at this time.

Working with bereaved children in school

Good communication with parents is essential to ensure that there is a real partnership in supporting bereaved children. If necessary, provide support for parents or find out where you can refer them.

Remember that school could be the only place where a child may be able to talk about their grief: conversely, school may be a place where the child feels insecure because a loved one has been left behind at home.

Younger children can be helped to identify and express how they are feeling through curriculum work such as drawing, circle time and responding to a story that has been read to them. Older children may appreciate the opportunity to talk things over with a caring adult who is not emotionally involved with the death. For the adolescent, school may present a challenge as grief can make it hard to concentrate – the emotional burden of grief may get in the way of effective learning. Emotions can already run high in adolescence and grief may make them even more intense; on the other hand, they might put all their energy into forgetting while at school.

Try to achieve a balance between allowing a bereaved child to express their feelings and ensuring that school can be a place of peace and normality away from any trauma at home. Set up structures that allow bereaved children access to appropriate adults in school whenever they feel the need, and access to a quiet place they can go to if things get too much. Do not overcompensate with too much attention, which may make the child feel different.

Sometimes another life event, such as moving home or a new step-parent, is the catalyst for delayed grief. Setting up support structures will help, such as working with the bereaved pupil's peer group, allowing the pupil access to speak to an adult in the school, and informing staff so they will be sensitive to the situation.

If a pupil has died, the rest of the class will be aware of the empty desk and coat-peg. Some schools will have talked to the class about this and may have decided together to keep them empty until the end of the school year when everything changes anyway.

Think about activities in school to help children deal with bereavement. Here are some examples:

- If it is a whole school bereavement, then a ritual of some kind can be organised to ensure that everyone can express their feelings and say goodbye.
- Prepare activities for children to help a bereaved child and to channel their own sad feelings.

- Prepare other pupils before a bereaved child comes back to school (see below).
- Make a school/class book as a memorial or as a gift to give to the bereaved family.
- Classmates or school friends could make cards to send home to the bereaved child or the child's parents.

To prepare pupils for a child's return to school, gather together the child's special friends and talk about how he or she might be feeling and what they might do to help. Depending on the circumstances, it might also be useful to talk to the child's class or even the whole school, maybe mentioning them in assembly. Arrange for a special friend or friends to meet the child before school or at the school gates so he or she doesn't have to enter the playground or classroom alone, and ensure that the child is not on their own throughout the first day or days.

Preparing the school community for someone dying

When a pupil or a member of staff dies it will naturally affect the whole school community. If the death is of a parent, then it will affect the pupil, the class teacher and most likely the pupil's school friends.

It is important to be aware that members of staff may be upset about the death and will have to deal with this as well as that of the the pupils they teach. Some might refrain from talking about the death to pupils because of their own issues or out of fear of upsetting the young people they teach. Teachers, however, are in a unique position to support bereaved pupils; they can be the trusted adult to turn to when a pupil needs to talk. The school and the classroom also offer structure and normality – an escape from the changes and upset at home.

Schools need to be prepared for various eventualities:

- the death of an adult working in the school;
- supporting a terminally ill pupil;
- supporting a pupil with a terminally ill family member;
- supporting a pupil who is grieving;
- cases of unexpected death, such as a fatal accident.

Having a policy that identifies these eventualities and offers procedures and strategies would be helpful in preparing a school for their management. The policy should identify: local agencies; a trained member of staff to consult; curriculum work; possible memorials; literature available for classroom and individual use; appropriate assemblies; and books and leaflets to be made available to parents.

Teachers and other professionals are often anxious about physically comforting an upset child. Every organisation that works with children and young people (including religious organisations) should have a child protection policy, and someone on the staff who is responsible for ensuring that it is implemented.

Any professional who is concerned about what is acceptable should refer to their organisation's policy and must ensure that this issue is discussed and understood by the whole staff.

Summary

- Support from family, friends, neighbours and organisations is very helpful for the child.

- Take your cue from the child; they may wish to talk about the death, or to use the opportunity of being with you to forget the trauma at home.

- Prepare other children by talking to them and suggesting ways in which they can help the bereaved child.

- The school community should have staff, pupil and curriculum policies in place for such eventualities.

CHAPTER 5

Helping children to grieve well

True love is a durable fire
In the mind ever burning.
Never sick, never old, never dead,
From itself never turning.

Sir Walter Raleigh

Grieving

Grieving is a necessary activity in the process of bereavement and, if a child is not given the opportunity at the time of the death, unresolved grief can stay with them for years, becoming more intense and dysfunctional.

In *Grief Counselling and Grief Therapy* (1983), William Worden wrote first about the four tasks of mourning:

1. To accept the reality of the loss.
2. To work through the grief.
3. To adjust to an environment in which the deceased is missing.
4. To withdraw emotional energy and reinvest it in another relationship.

This is not to say that the dead person is forgotten but, by working through grief, the mourner is able to accept the painful reality of the death and be comforted by fond memories. The journey through the four tasks of mourning may take months or years; for some people it will never be completed.

Some children's ability to verbalise and express feelings may be limited. While grieving, the child will be experiencing many feelings and their behaviour, whether withdrawn or aggressive, may be the only indication as to what they may be feeling. It is therefore most important that children are given the opportunity to process and express their feelings. This is sometimes called grief work.

This section is full of ideas and strategies that adults can use with children in the weeks and months after experiencing a death.

Through these activities the child will be able to:

- talk through and treasure memories;
- process and express strong feelings;
- come to terms with what has happened.

Adults working with a child in this way may also be mourning. There will probably be upset feelings on both sides, maybe tears. Hopefully, some laughter might accompany these and certainly some understanding and sense of relief.

It is never too late to do any of these activities and they are helpful to adults as well as children.

A collage of photographs

Looking through photographs and remembering happier times can be therapeutic. A useful piece of grief work can be collecting a number of photographs and cutting them out to make a collage, which a child can then have in their room. The activity of making a collage will evoke a lot of feelings and memories of special times and the collage itself will be something to treasure.

Ten good times

Make a booklet with writing and drawings of ten good times the child spent with the deceased. This can follow on from the previous activity.

Special things

A child can be helped to remember special things about the person who has died, such as: things they liked to eat; places they enjoyed visiting; favourite flowers, music, pictures and books; favourite activities, such as feeding the birds, making cakes, playing football; the clothes they liked to wear.

The child could make a drawing of the person and then write the special things all round the figure. He or she could go further, such as preparing a special meal with the person's favourite foods or doing something the child had done and enjoyed with the person.

Poetry, painting, writing and music

Being able to express oneself in writing, drawing, painting or playing music can be a very helpful creative outlet. The adult does not have to be a therapist to encourage this; the important thing is to be able to offer the opportunity or give the idea to the child in a non-directive way.

Useful websites

There are suggestions of useful websites for children and young people on page 94. Some are for the child to use alone and some are best used with the adult, so it would be helpful for the adult to have a look at them before suggesting their use, and also to ensure that they are relevant to the particular child's age and ability.

Some of the websites provide the facility for children to add their own poems, drawings and writing.

A memory box or suitcase of memories

The adult can help the child to find a large box or suitcase and maybe decorate it. The child can put inside reminders of their special person:

- photographs;
- drawings;
- CDs/tapes/videos;
- special objects that belonged to the person, such as hats, gloves, keys, jewellery, buttons, perfume, aftershave, spectacles, a favourite pen, material from a familiar dress, a tie;
- reminders of special times, such as pressed flowers, seashells, postcards, birthday cards, luggage labels from a holiday, an old passport;
- a sample of the person's handwriting;
- an old diary of the person;
- a favourite book or piece of music;
- pictures of favourite foods;

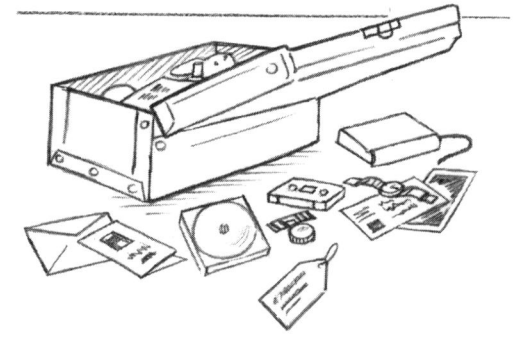

- a letter the child would write if the person were still alive;
- the newspaper announcement of the death, a service sheet from the funeral, cards and letters received at the time of the death;
- a short life story of the person who died;
- a family tree.

The contents of the box can be added to over months or even years and a child may want to talk to other relatives and friends to add to their memories, stories or special objects. The initial making of the box and consequent looking through it can be very comforting to a child and something to treasure as they become an adult.

Writing a biography

This is a good way for the child to find out more about the dead person. It will be a way of keeping his or her memory alive and having a permanent reminder of the person. When they are older they may be able to share this with their own children. It is a means of talking to friends and relatives and maybe breaking any 'barriers of silence' that can descend on conversations about the person who has died.

It could include:

- the life story from birth to death;
- important dates;
- the person's hobbies, achievements and special interests;
- the person's friends and relatives;
- the person's personality – the good and not so good aspects!
- special times and memories;
- a family tree;
- illnesses and how the person died;
- the funeral – what happened, who came, special words that were said.

Grandma was one of three children
She used to live in London
She taught me how to knit

Compiling a life path

A life path is a simpler way than a biography of compiling the story of the person who died. A significant event is recorded on each step of the pathway.

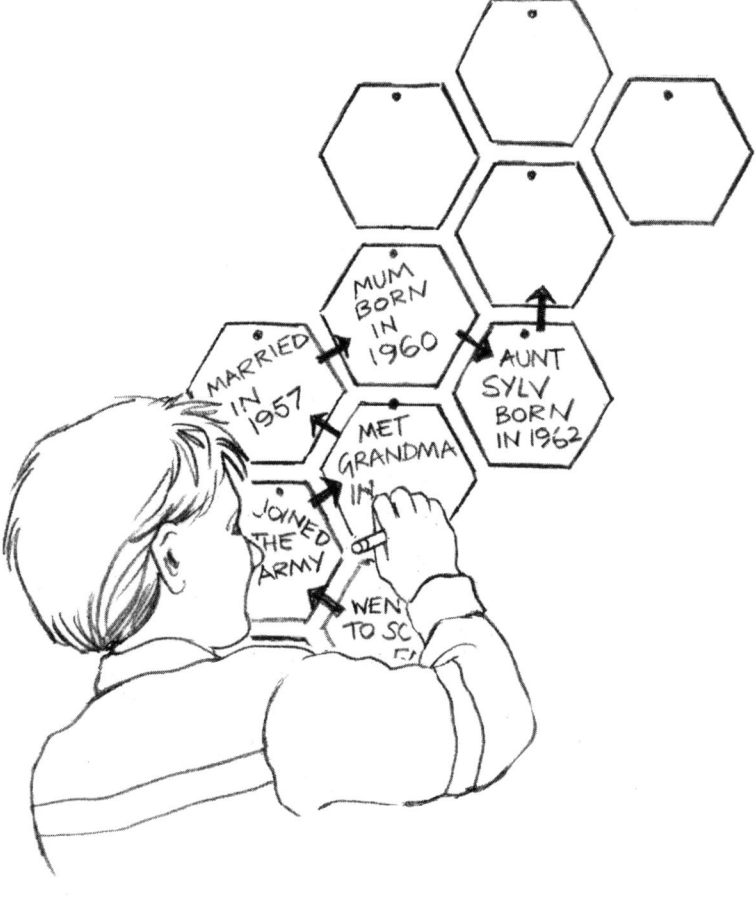

MUM BORN IN 1960

AUNT SYLV BORN IN 1962

MARRIED IN 1957

MET GRANDMA IN

JOINED THE ARMY

WEN TO SC

Making a family tree

Making a family tree is a good way of understanding the continuity of life and how people belong to a network of others who live and die. This activity gives another opportunity to talk to other members of the family and share memories and stories.

Story reading and telling

There are many stories for children of all ages concerning death and grieving. These can be accessed through the library service, the internet or bookshops. Most good bookshops and libraries will be able to advise on appropriate literature. The local school library service may be another source of information to access books on death and grief.

Having books available to be read to children or for them to read themselves may help them recognise that they are not alone. A story can also be the 'way in' to discuss feelings or share memories.

Difficult things for me now

Write 'Difficult Things For Me Now' on the centre of a page. Working with the child, help to identify all the difficult things that the child might be experiencing, such as everyone being sad at home, mealtimes and seeing a parent upset.

Things that help

Use the same technique but this time identify things that help the child, such as looking at photographs, playing music, writing things down, playing with friends, having a cuddle and being with their pet.

Summary

- Grieving is a healing activity in the bereavement process.
- Children need to be given the opportunity to identify, process and express their feelings.
- Grief work can be therapeutic and enables the child to think and talk about treasured memories.
- Some of the things created in this section may prove to be very special as the child grows into adulthood.

CHAPTER 6

Remembering

She is gone
You can shed tears that she is gone
or you can smile because she has lived.
You can close your eyes and pray that she'll come back
or you can open your eyes and see all she's left.
Your heart can be empty because you can't see her
or you can be full of the love you shared.
You can turn your back on tomorrow and live yesterday
or you can be happy for tomorrow because of yesterday.
You can remember her and only that she's gone
or you can cherish her memory and let it live on.
You can cry and close your mind, be empty and turn your back
or you can do what she'd want: smile, open your eyes, love and go
on.

Anonymous

Different traditions of remembering

Many faiths and cultures have ways of remembering the dead
person after the funeral or to mark the anniversary of the person's
death. Jews, Muslims and Christians often mark their graves with a
headstone with the person's name and some inscription.

Christians sometimes hold a memorial service in church a few
weeks after the funeral. Some churches invite people to light candles
in church in memory of the dead person or invite families to pay for
flowers in church once a year. Others will say prayers on the
anniversary of the death.

Orthodox Christians may have a service for the dead and invite
people by giving them a loaf of bread. During the service, a special
food, similar to porridge, is given to everyone as a symbol of new
life. Each person takes a little of this and says 'May God forgive'.
They believe that when someone dies, their spirit has no need for
food any more and giving away food helps the soul to move on to a
spiritual life.

Latin American countries celebrate the Day of the Dead, a tradition the Roman Catholic church has adopted. People place flowers, gifts, food and drink on family graves and families often have picnics at the graveside, saying prayers for the person's soul. In Britain, All Saints' Day – traditionally when the Christian church remembers those who have died – is no longer widely observed, whereas the commercialised Halloween, when children dress up as skeletons, witches and ghouls, is celebrated by many families.

Muslims read the Quaran right through as a gift to the dead. They often split up sections for different members of the family to read.

In the synagogue, the rabbi will read out the dead person's name on the anniversary of the death and relatives light a special long-burning candle called a *yahrzest* and say the *kadish* – the Jewish mourner's prayer.

Buddists give away food and money on the anniversary of a death.

Hindus will have a shrine at home for the dead person and will light incense and candles and say prayers for the dead person.

People therefore have a tradition of giving money to charity, setting up funds in the name of the dead person, lighting candles, remembering with prayers, and having somewhere to go, either at home, in a religious building or at a graveside. Organisations or places of work may donate money for a special memorial such as a picture, plaque or seat, and schools often remember a pupil or member of staff with a special prize or award or a named bench in the playground, by planting a tree or by creating a special wild garden. Some people invite family and friends to put a light on a tree at Christmas time and to gather round with mince pies and a drink.

Some undertakers and hospices have yearly gatherings for relatives and friends of the deceased and most crematoriums hold annual memorial services.

Activities for children to remember special people

For children, as with adults, there will be difficult days when they might miss their particular people who have died more deeply, such as birthdays, Christmas and other religious festivals, the anniversary of the death and mothers' and fathers' days. It is important for children and young people to be able to recognise these days in a special way and to have a place they can go to or an activity they can do for comfort. The opposite of this is a day where everyone remembers but nothing is said – rather like in the poem 'Small Talk' on page 11.

It is good, therefore, for families to be prepared for these days and to talk to children about special ways in which they can all remember their loved one. It will be helpful for all concerned to do something special together. If this is not possible, other adults working with the child can help the child remember in a simple and special way.

A celebration meal

The family could plan a special meal comprising the favourite foods of their person. Each member of the family could help in the preparations, such as writing a simple prayer or speech to say at the table, decorating placemats, picking flowers to put round a photograph and choosing or playing special music.

Making a memory garden

Having a small patch of garden in memory of the person can be special for a child. It is an easily accessible place for a child to go to if they are feeling the need to remember or to be quiet. The child can be helped to prepare the garden, decide what to plant and observe the cycle of nature.

'My father, when he was dying, asked if the snowdrops were out. When he died I started to plant snowdrops and every year when I see them grow again I am reminded of him.'

Flowers can be picked and placed by a photograph. Messages can be buried in the garden or tied to a branch. There can be decorations at times such as birthdays.

Decorations at different festivals

The child can be involved in placing special lights or decorations on the Christmas tree or round a shrine or special place in the house in memory of the dead person.

Lighting candles

A candle lit at home on significant days to remember a loved one can be very healing. Adults should ensure that this is safe and that the child is able to place flowers, pieces of writing or messages nearby if they wish.

Visiting the graveside or the crematorium

Visiting the place where the remains of the body were placed can be comforting for some people and tending the ground or placing flowers might be helpful for children. Each crematorium has a book of remembrance that records the name and date of the death of all those who had a funeral ceremony there. On that day each year it will be open at that page and available for viewing. Given prior notice, a crematorium is able to tell a family where the remains were placed, if there is no marker. Crematoriums also hold annual memorial services.

Using the memory box

The memory box or suitcase (see page 73), once put together, can be very helpful on these difficult days. A child should be able to look at the contents and maybe add to them. Photographs, videos and music could be shared with the family. If an adult looks through it with a child it might prompt other memories to share.

Making a skyscape of memories

Winston's Wish is a national organisation that provides services for grieving children and their families. In the 'Remember' section of its website (see page 94), there is a sky with stars and planets where children can introduce their own named star and read other children's messages on other stars. This will help them see that they are not alone, and they can visit the website and read, update or change their message whenever they wish. Children also have the opportunity to post poems or writing on the site or post a picture with a message of remembrance.

Giving gifts

Children say that they find the birthdays of the person who has died difficult because they cannot give gifts. Families could instead give a charity gift, sponsor a child in a Third World country or make up a shoe box for a Romanian child as a special present in memory. Children could write a message on a balloon and let it go or make a card or write a message to put in the memory box or a designated place of their own.

Having a day out

Instead of being sad and mournful for the day, a positive way to spend a difficult anniversary is to plan something pleasant to do or a fun day out. Most people would say that their loved one would not want them to be sad and mournful and

'For years after our mother's death, my sister and I would have a "Brenda Brown Memorial Shopping Spree" day. It seemed such an appropriate way to remember her!'

doing something together as a family will help to support each other and get through the day.

Being still

Some children and young people may just want to be quiet and still on their own. They might want to find a place where they can be undisturbed and remember in their own way. Teenagers in particular often spend time away from the rest of the family and this will include times for remembering.

Summary

- Difficult days and anniversaries need planning for.
- Activities for remembering can be comforting.

CHAPTER 7

Memo from a grieving child

Please:

- Keep me informed of what is going on.
- Be honest with me, even if you have to say 'I don't know'.
- Speak in simple language with no euphemisms.
- Let me be involved in the grieving process with others – don't exclude me.
- Let me cry alongside you.
- Let me be able to comfort others.
- Assure me that I am loved and safe and will be taken care of.
- Accept what I do or say without judgement – don't compare me with others.
- Let me be able to say goodbye.
- Allow me to talk freely about the person who has died.
- Give me the structure, discipline and routine that will help me recover.
- Help me to keep the memories alive.

Useful contacts

The Child Bereavement Trust
Website: www.childbereavement.org.uk

The Child Bereavement Trust is a national charity that networks in order to assist families and professionals in accessing suitable agencies in their own area. It offers information, publications and training for professionals. The website includes information for bereaved families, young people and professionals.

Cruse
Website: www.crusebereavementcare.org.uk

Cruse provides counselling and support for all ages. It offers advice, education and training services. The website includes a section on bereavement and helping children, as well as information for schools and professionals.

Winston's Wish
Website: www.winstonswish.org.uk

Winston's Wish is a charity offering support, information and guidance to bereaved children and young people up to 18 years old and their families.

Helplines
Cruse
Day-by-day helpline: 0870 167 1677
Email: helpline@crusebereavementcare.org.uk
Young people's helpline: 0808 808 1677

Winston's Wish
Helpline for families and professionals: 0845 203 0405

Websites for children and young people

The Child Bereavement Trust
Website: www.childbereavement.org.uk, click on For Young People

Information and advice for teenagers on many aspects of bereavement. Teenagers are also invited to ask questions and add their stories, feelings and poems.

Cruse – Road for You
Website: rd4u.org.uk

This website aims to enable each teenager who accesses it to find their own 'road' in dealing with their loss. It includes: personal experiences along a time line; dealing with emotions; an interactive message board; a fun zone; and a 'lads only' section.

NSPCC
Website: there4me.com

This website is for teenagers and offers confidential advice and help on any problem.

Riprap – when a Parent has Cancer
Website: www.riprap.org.uk

A website for young people that identifies emotions, shares stories of other young people going through similar experiences, and gives information and facts. Young people can also email questions, ask for advice and give feedback.

Winston's Wish
Website: www.winstonswish.org.uk, click on For Young People

A bright, helpful website where children can click on See, Talk, Ask, Play, Say, Try. It includes: games; answers to frequently asked questions; a chat room for young people to talk to each other about their experiences; a forum for poems, thoughts, songs, pictures and drawings; and ideas for remembering, including creating one's own star in Skyscape.

Index

Acknowledgements

Adaptation of *Waterbugs and Dragonflies: Explaining Death to Young Children* by Doris Stickney, Copyright © 2002 by Continuum International Publishing Group. Reproduced by kind permission of Continuum International Publishing Group.

Adaptation of *Watership Down* by Richard Adams, Copyright © 1974 by Richard Adams. Reprinted with permission of David Higham Associates Ltd, London.

Extract from *Harry Potter & The Philosopher's Stone* by J.K. Rowling, Copyrigh t © 1997 J.K. Rowling. Reprinted with permission of Christopher Little Literary Agency, London.

'Small Talk' by Guy Perkins, Copyright © 2007 Guy Perkins.

'Verse 21' from *The Fugitive* by Rabindranath Tagore. Reprinted with permission of Visva-Bharati University.